The
SCOTS GUARDS

The Guard of Honour was founded by the Second Battalion Scots Guards when Her Majesty The Queen arrived at Waverley Station, Edinburgh, on her first visit to Scotland following her coronation at Westminster Abbey in June 1953.

Front Cover: Lance Sergeant Heriot and Lance Corporal Dunning were photographed at Auchincruive College, near Ayr, in 2001 on the occasion of their visit to the Ayr Branch of the Scots Guards Association.

Back Cover: Falkland Palace, Fife. This photograph shows members of the Scots Guards Recruiting Team which covered Scotland in 1972, under the charge of Major Tony Philipson. It will be seen that the team is visiting Falkland Palace, which has had a close connection with the Regiment since 1650. The palace was a favourite seat of the Scottish Court since the reign of King James V. His daughter Mary Queen of Scots hunted from here. Charles I and Charles II also visited the palace.

A Scots Guards Piper is seen at the window and a Guardsman is seen near the entrance.

The palace is now under the care of the National Trust for Scotland to which we are grateful for the loan of this picture.

The
SCOTS GUARDS

William F. Hendrie & Jack Smith

TEMPUS

Dedicated to
every Scots Guardsman
past and present.

First published 2002
Copyright © William F. Hendrie and Jack Smith, 2002

Tempus Publishing Limited
The Mill, Brimscombe Port,
Stroud, Gloucestershire, GL5 2QG
www.tempus-publishing.com

ISBN 0 7524 2399 1

TYPESETTING AND ORIGINATION BY
Tempus Publishing Limited
PRINTED IN GREAT BRITAIN BY
Midway Colour Print, Wiltshire

Contents

Foreword

This is a unique book: I do not think that anyone before has produced such a collection of photographs devoted to the various periods in the history of the Scots Guards, very many of which I had never seen before despite my long service with the Regiment.

Certainly it has involved Jack Smith, formerly of the Scots Guards, in co-operation with William F. Hendrie, in a considerable amount of hard work searching for and selecting material. The pictures illustrate clearly our roles in peace and war, and in ceremonial and operational duties. They also show the family spirit which we all share, bound together by a common pride until we die and bearing a motto which the Royal Grandfather of Her Majesty The Queen, our Colonel-In-Chief, once translated thus:

Beware of challenging the Scots Guards.

General Sir Michael Gow

General Sir Michael Gow, GCB, DL, enlisted into the Scots Guards in 1942. When he retired in 1968 he was the Senior General in the Army and the last member of the Armed Forces to have served during the Second World War. He served at every level in the Army, including Guardsman. He commanded in Battalion, Brigade, Division and Army Group levels. He was Governor of Edinburgh Castle. His final command was Commandant of the Royal College of Defence Studies, London.

Acknowledgements

There are many photographs to be found in history books and magazines which portray the Scots Guards and there are many more in the archives, but the majority of the pictures which appear in this book have come from individuals who are proud of their connection with this very famous Regiment and who have had relatives who have been guardsmen. My thanks to all those who have helped to make possible the publication of this book by loaning photographs or providing help in other ways. Special thanks go to General Sir Michael Gow for his encouragement and the Edinburgh and Lothian Branch of the Scots Guards Association for their support throughout this entire venture. In particular, my thanks to Branch Secretary Danny Minto, Captain Hay of the Army Careers Information Office, Edinburgh Castle, and the National Trust for Scotland for permission to reproduce the photo of Falkland Palace.

This book has been produced to mark the Golden Jubilee of the succession to the throne of Her Majesty Queen Elizabeth, who is Colonel-In-Chief of the Regiment, and it is therefore fitting that many of the illustrations show events during the period leading up to and following her coronation in June 1953.

'Never have I seen in men's faces such strength of character,' declared Sir Winston Churchill to the Commanding Officer of the Third (Tank) Battalion of the Scots Guards after he inspected them during the Second World War. On looking through this book, I feel certain readers will appreciate what the great British wartime leader meant.

Jack Smith

One
1642 to 1918

The Scots Guards' badge depicts the star of the Order of the Thistle set upon the Saltire or St Andrew's Cross, whose bars are separated by heraldic rays. Officers and warrant officers wear silver badges while non-commissioned officers and guardsmen wear brass badges and the insignia also appears on all uniform buttons. The motto of the Scots Guards is *Nemo me impune lacessit*, which translated from Latin into English means 'Touch me not with impunity', or more dramatically in Scots, 'Wha daur meddle wi' me'!

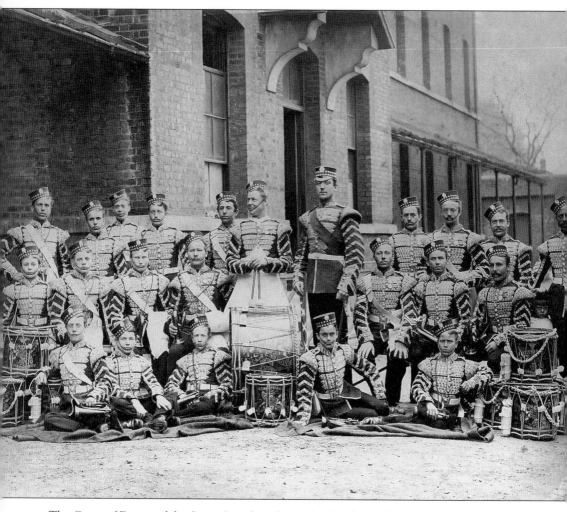

The Corps of Drums of the Scots Guards make a splendid show when this early photograph was taken in 1881. From the time the Regiment was founded in 1642 by the first Marquis of Argyll at the request of King Charles I as independent companies to safeguard the King's interests in Ireland, the Scots Guards have always marched to the music of the Corps of Drums and answered to the call of the bugles, which the drummers also carry and play. The band also includes fife players. The Regiment has also always been associated with the pipes, the officers originally paying for their own pipers, recalling the old saying, 'He who pays the piper calls the tune'! The pipers were formally authorised as an official part of the Regiment in 1856 and the pipe band was formed in 1870. The drum major in the picture alone amongst the men wears a peaked cap, while the bandsmen all wear pill box hats. In time of war the drummers always served as stretcher bearers.

A wide hat and breeches are noticeable features of the earliest Scots Guards uniform, which this drawing shows as it was worn in 1684. The wearing of uniform was a seventeenth-century innovation. The Highland Company of the Scots Guards wore Highland dress of kilt and plaid. Early battles at which the Scots Guards fought included Namur, Dettingen and Fontenoy.

MUSKETEER 1684

BATTALION COMPANY 1742 GRENADIER COMPANY

Half a century later in 1742 the uniform of the Scots Guards was as depicted in this sketch.

LIGHT COMPANY, 1793

Further changes took place as the eighteenth century progressed and this is how a Scots Guardsman appeared in 1793.

1807

OFFICER   PRIVATE

By the beginning of the nineteenth century the uniform looked as shown in this sketch depicting it in 1807.

At the Battle of Waterloo, where Napoleon and the French army were defeated in 1815, the Scots Guards uniform had assumed this appearance. The bravery shown by the Scots Guards made the British victory at Waterloo one of the Regiment's finest hours. The Regiment also fought at several of the previous battles during the Peninsula Campaign in Spain and Portugal.

1834
COLOUR
SERGEANT

1837
FLANK COMPANY
PRIVATE

Uniforms worn by the Scots Guards in 1834 and 1837 are shown in these two drawings.

11

The Scots Guards gained further battle honours during the 1854-1856 Crimean War. Shortly after their arrival in the Crimea the guardsmen staunchly defended the colours at the Battle of Alma. Four of the first Victoria Crosses were bravely earned during this campaign. The uniforms worn by the Scots Guards during the Crimean War are depicted in this display at the Regiment's museum at Wellington Barracks.

Opposite: This famous oil painting captures the moment when Sergeant Fraser of the Scots Guards courageously dismounted a French officer from his horse and rode it back to Hougmount Farm, which the Regiment was defending along with the Coldstream Guards. The defence of Hougmount Farm by the Guards at Waterloo proved a vitally important turning point in the course of the day-long battle.

SERGEANT-MAJOR 1891

Left: A sergeant major in the uniform worn by the Scots Guards at around the period of the Boer War when the Regiment sailed 6,000 miles to fight in South Africa.

Below: At the Guards Depot at Caterham, twenty-one men completed training from a squad of about thirty who had joined the Regiment on 1 November 1907. This represented the average wastage. The men in the photograph are, from left to right, back row: Lingfield, Lingley, Conlan. Second Row: McKenzie, Williamson, Shepherd, -?-, Boyd, Davidson, Lewis. Third Row: Henderson, Milne, Leatherhead, Corporal Lamb, -?-, Mclean, Loley, Robertson. Front Row: Langley, Arthur, Turner, Colour Sergeant Strang, Sergeant Robbie, -?-, Reid, Blandell, Birtless. The two Guardsmen in bearskins were already fully trained soldiers. The pillbox caps had not yet been replaced by peaked caps. All of the men are also wearing polished leather leggings.

The men of M Company, Second Battalion Scots Guards were pictured here marching in the Evelyn Wood Competition held in 1908.

During the First World War three battalions of the Scots Guards fought on the Western Front. This photograph shows the commanding officer of the Third Battalion with his staff officers pictured on the steps of the Guards Chapel at the Regiment's headquarters at Wellington Barracks, Birdcage Walk, adjacent to Buckingham Palace. On the extreme left is Sergeant McNess VC and on the extreme right are Captain G.A. Boyd-Rochfort VC, and Sergeant J. McAulay VC, DCM.

Sergeant Veale's Squad was photographed at the Guards Depot, Caterham in 1916. Both the first and second battalions of the Scots Guards fought on the Western Front from 1914 until the Armistice on 11 November 1918. The First Battalion left the UK in August 1914 as part of the First Brigade of the First Division, the original British Expeditionary Force, which was known as the 'old Contemptibles', took part in the hard-fought defensive battles at the beginning of the war. The Second Battalion in its turn left the UK in October 1914 as part of the Twentieth Brigade and Seventh Division. During the four years of the First World War the Scots Guards were awarded thirty-one battle honours while members of the Regiment were decorated with five Victoria Crosses. One hundred and eleven officers and 2,730 other ranks, the equivalent of three battalions, gave their lives for their country.

Two
The 1930s

The First Battalion of the Scots Guards was stationed at Tweedledown Camp, Colchester, in Essex during the 1930s. The Corps of Drums are seen on parade in this photograph taken in 1934.

Top: The Corps of Drums appears again in this photograph along with the pipe band of the Battalion leaving the camp at Colchester. It is interesting to note that the drums are of the old-fashioned variety known as guards' drums, used before the introduction of rod tension drums.

Bottom: On return to Tweedledown Camp, the men attended to their drums and cleaned their webbing as seen in this informal picture. The drummers included Hunt, Lee, Hamilton, Lucos, and Harradine. Twelve men slept in each tent and also had to find space for all of their kit, rifles and instruments.

Opposite top: The Battalion pipers were photographed relaxing after an exercise. The white bands on their Glengarries indicated that they had played the role of the enemy. Lance Corporal Bright, Piper Robertson and Piper Couttes are in the foreground.

The First Battalion commanded by Lieutenant Colonel Swinton was ordered to sail to Egypt in 1935 because of the threat posed by Italy's threat to take over Abyssinia. On 1 November the Regiment was photographed embarking on the Bibby Line troopship, SS *Somersetshire*. They landed at Alexandria on 15 November and were stationed nine miles east of the port at Sidi Bishr Camp, where they lived under canvas. In December Left Flank and one platoon of S. Company, which was the machine gun company, commanded by Major H.L. Graham, transferred to Mersa Matruh in order to reinforce the garrison there. This small port on the coast on the northern edge of the desert was about one hundred and fifty miles from the frontier with Libya.

After arrival in Egypt the pipe band of the Scots Guards were pictured playing during the General Officer Commanding's inspection at the barracks in Cairo.

The hot climate of Egypt made hygiene even more essential than usual and here men of the Regiment are seen swabbing the floor of their barrack room. This duty was carried out every Saturday morning before the CO's inspection.

Kasr-el-nil Barracks was described by the men of the Scots Guards as 'simply lousy' and debugging was an essential routine exercise. Beds were taken to bits at least three times every week and blow lamps were used to exterminate the insects. Doors and windows were sealed and all kit was carefully stored indoors but even these precautions failed to entirely eliminate the problem. The Hilton Hotel now stands on the site which the barracks occupied!

The Scots Guards provided the Guard of Honour for the funeral of King Fuad and for the accession of his successor King Farouk. This photograph shows the Scots Guards on parade again with Regimental colours at the dip for the salute when the new monarch paid his first visit to the British High Commissioner, Sir Miles Lampson. The men are seen presenting arms.

Sir George Weir GOC inspected the First Battalion in Cairo in 1936.

The Corps of Drums under Drum Major Watts.

Scots Guards pipers under Pipe Major A. MacDonald. In the front are seen Colonel A. Swinton MC, DSO, and Lieutenant-Adjutant C. I. Dunbar.

The men of the Battalion Corporals' Mess pictured in 1936.

The Battalion moved in 1936 to Mersa Matruh near Alexandria. Travel was by train and this photograph shows piled arms and kitbags stacked ready to be put on board.

Haversack rations were issued for the long thirsty journey.

The Battalion spent two months at Montrose Camp, Mersa Matruh. Much of their time was spent digging trenches in the sand in order to provide defences.

Digging trenches in the desert was a most difficult task as the loose sand and vicious sand storms made the job impossible. Fortunately problems with Libya lessened by the end of March and their Battalion withdrew to Cairo, where it took over from the Third Battalion Grenadier Guards at Kasr-el-nil Barracks.

Another journey undertaken by the Battalion in 1936 was by sea. It was a most unpleasant experience because of the condition of the ship the *Zaffaron*. The Scots Guardsmen had replaced a cargo of live animals and no effort had been made to clean the decks. Lieutenant Colonel Swinton refused to allow his men on board until the whole vessel was disinfected.

Piper Magheacon was pictured disembarking from the voyage on the *Zaffaron*.

This early model of Bren Gun carrier was used during the Scots Guards stay in Egypt. The Regiment had only given up its horses and become motorised a short time before leaving UK for Egypt and the first vehicles provided many teething problems during their period overseas.

The Scots Guards pipes and drums beat retreat at Montrose Camp, Mersa Matruh, in 1936 before sailing home on RMS *Laurentic*, which sailed from Port Said and reached Southampton on 7 December 1936.

The men of Sergeant Jack Richmond's Squad at initial training are seen wearing khaki with diced peak caps and white webbing at Caterham in 1938. The white webbing was abolished during the Second World War. Sergeant Richmond was decorated with the Military Medal.

The drummers of the Scots Guards took part in the famous Aldershot tattoo in 1938.

Three

The Second World War

This photograph shows the Third Tank Battalion Scots Guards. Although trained and expert as infantry men, the men of the Battalion were surprised to learn in May 1941 that they were to convert to become an armoured Battalion. They left Chigwell on 16 September for Tilshead Camp, near Salisbury, where they joined the Guards Armoured Division and the Sixth Guards Armoured Brigade. The Battalion subsequently transferred to B Camp, Codford St Mary, on the edge of Salisbury Plain and reminded there until April 1943, when it moved north to the Hawes district of Yorkshire. Before moving from Codford, the Battalion was inspected by HRH The Duke of Gloucester, who presented the Commander of each tank with a pennant in the Guards Brigade colours to be flown on the wireless aerials of their Churchill Tanks. These new tanks performed better than previous models.

The Officers, Third Tank Battalion, Scots Guards posed for this photograph in March 1943. There are several well kent faces amongst the officers including the Rev. T.B. Reid, who was later the Moderator of the Church of Scotland, Major W.S.I. Whitelaw, who later became Home Secretary in the Conservative Government, and 2nd Lieutenant R.A.K. Runcie, later Archbishop of Canterbury.

Corporal Poulton's Squad was photographed at the Guards Depot, Caterham, in 1943. Sergeant Leatch, the PT Instructor wearing the white vest in the centre of the picture, served twenty-seven years with the Regiment and on his retiral became a Beefeater at the Tower of London.

Officers training at the Royal Military College, Sandhurst, were pictured with an early model of a Bren Gun Carrier.

The officers of the Scots Guards with the Duke of Gloucester.

A Scots Guards Officer is seen with his gas mask while training at the Royal Military College in 1940.

Officer John Young while training at Sandhurst.

Admiring this sow in the pigsty brought a light-hearted moment during training at Sandhurst. This picture was taken by Major Alister Ritchie.

Officers Miles, Willeybry and Webster also stopped to admire the sow in the pig sty which promised plenty of rashers for breakfast despite wartime rationing. They were fellow students of Major Alister Ritchie at Sandhurst.

A bomb crater at the Royal Military College, Sandhurst.

Meanwhile, in July 1942, the Second Battalion was fighting in Egypt. They suffered many casualties in the Western Depot. Their losses were due to the fact that they would fight to the last! In the German General Rommel's assessment of them he said, 'Almost a living embodiment of the virtues and faults of the British soldier – tremendous courage and tenacity combined with a lack of mobility.'

Although there are only eight graves of Scots Guardsmen in the El Alamein Cemetery (most are in Libya), the town is significant in the history of the Scots Guards because it features as a Battle of Honour (in defence of the Alamein Line). It also marks the end of a phase in the Second Battalion's actions in North Africa.

Seen in this photograph is one of the Scots Guards graves at El Alamein Cemetery.

12th Platoon, C Company at Sandhurst.

This young officers drill class was pictured at the Training Battalion Scots Guards, Pirbright.

His Majesty King George VI inspected the Fourth Battalion of the Scots Guards at the Royal School at Wanstead in November 1941. He later watched the men undertake an assault course and gave the men great encouragement. He was particularly interested as two months earlier on 28 September, His Majesty had granted approval for the formation of the Fourth Battalion Scots Guards at a time when there was a great influx of men into the army. The Fourth Battalion had a short difficult life supplying recruits for the other three Battalions.

The Fourth Battalion Headquarters Company of the Scots Guard were photographed on parade at Wanstead.

Company Quarter Master Sergeant Bradley pictured in Essex in 1942 while training with W Company, Fourth Battalion.

The grenade range in Essex where Fourth Battalion practised.

Early in 1942 the Battalion moved from Wanstead to North Devon for battle training on Exmoor. The men experienced a hard time as they were accommodated in tents and the rocky surface made it difficult to drive in pegs with which to secure them. A subsequent gale flattened the whole camp and the Company records and officers' mess accounts were blown away. This photograph shows the cookhouse.

Establishing the camp in North Devon.

Men at the camp in North Devon.

Officers at the camp in North Devon.

Working at the camp in North Devon.

There was also time however to relax at the battle training camp in North Devon.

Guardsmen Williams and McNab were pictured while taking part in cliff climbing exercises in North Devon.

Guardsman Dudgeon also took part in the cliff climbing exercise at Woolacombe in North Devon in May 1942.

*Above:*On patrol during Exercise Pigeon at Frome, Somerset, in June 1942. On the right is Sergeant Young.

*Left:*Guardsmen pictured during Exercise Pigeon. Sadly during this exercise Lance Sergeant J. Porter and Guardsman N. Hughey were drowned during river crossings.

This photograph submitted by Mrs J. Bennie from Forfar is believed to have been taken in Egypt while the Second Battalion was stationed in Cairo. It shows her brother, Guardsman Cuthbert, (Bert) Peddie crouching at the front of this happy relaxed off duty group. Sadly Cuthbert Bennie was later killed in action at the Battle of Salerno on 10 September 1943. On that day the Battalion was attacking what the men wrongly called the Tobacco Factory. It was in fact a large storage warehouse for tinned food. In addition to Guardsmen Peddie several other members of the Battalion lost their lives. Since the war Mrs Bennie has visited the war graves at Salerno on several occasions.

Scots Guards officers were pictured in relaxed mood as they strolled through the Square at Wellington Barracks which can be seen in the background.

The men of the Scots Guards are seen in this photograph while training at Holkham in Norfolk in May 1943.

Above: The Norfolk exercise involved boat training.

Left: This further scene was also taken during the boat training exercises.

On exercise in Norfolk in May 1943.

Boat training on the Norfolk Broads.

Manning the boats while undergoing training on the Norfolk Broads in May 1943.

The tank of the General Officer Commanding during an exercise on the Yorkshire Wolds in December 1943.

The view from the tanks of the large flat training area on the Yorkshire Wolds.

The tanks in Yorkshire in December 1943.

Although by then a vehicle Battalion with an armoured division with tanks, the Scots Guards never lost their love of horses as seen here in this photograph of Major Ritchie taken at Brompton near Scarborough on Boxing Day 1943.

The Scots Guards took part in the Normandy Landings in June 1944. X Company of the Fourth Battalion had become an independent company attached to the Third Battalion Irish Guards. From Netley Common near Southampton they embarked on the Union Castle liner *Llangibby Castle*. For three days they lay at anchor off the Isle of Wight until on the morning of 23 June they landed at the famous Mulberry Harbour at Arromanches to begin their service in the recapture of Europe from the Germans.

A tank-landing craft at the Normandy beach head.

A German coastal defence gun in Normandy pictured following the capture of the beach.

Guardsman Lamont of X Company Scots Guards with a German tank which he helped capture.

David Lloyd was photographed digging in after landing in Normandy in June 1944.

After the sweaty task of digging in David Lloyd was pictured at ablutions.

The Guards Armoured Division crossing the Green Gap on its way to Caen.

This railway bridge had been blown up by the retreating Germans.

The Scots Guards moving up into the French town of Beauvais on 31 August 1944.

Scots Guards photographed walking along a street in Beauvais.

From the bridge head in France the Scots Guards moved forward into Belgium and were pictured there at the border crossing on 3 September 1944. Colonel Walter Sale is seen here at the frontier.

X Company took prisoners in Belgium.

A self-propelled seventeen-pounder gun pictured during the campaign in Belgium.

Adding a domestic detail, Company Sergeant Major Law and Company Quarter Master Sergeant Morrison were pictured in the cookhouse of X Company as the Regiment moved forward once again into Brussels.

The Scots Guards received a warm welcome when they liberated Brussels.

The Guards Armoured Division was photographed here moving into the Belgium Capital.

Crowds lined the streets of Brussels to welcome the tanks of the Guards Armoured Division.

A close-up of one of the tanks.

A Scots Guard dispatch rider was practically overwhelmed by the enthusiastic welcome which he received when he drove on his motor cycle into the heart of Brussels.

Belgium civilians joined Scots Guardsmen to celebrate the liberation of Brussels.

The final parade of X Company, Scots Guards with the First Battalion of the Welsh Guards at Nijmegen in the Netherlands on 17 March 1945, prior to rejoining the Second Battalion Scots Guards.

Above: Finally the Second Battalion Scots Guards had the satisfaction of reaching Germany itself and this scene was taken at Cuxhaven at the mouth of the River Elbe in May 1945.

Left: Members of the Second Battalion at Cuxhaven on 7 May 1945 after VE Day.

Right Flank Second Battalion of the Scots Guards on 10 May proceeded to Heligoland on a commandeered German mine sweeper to take the surrender of the German fortress on the island.

Aboard the commandeered German mine sweeper en route for Heligoland off the north-east coast of Germany.

On the voyage to Heligoland.

The submarine pens at Heligoland.

The Company Officer of the Scots Guards with Admiral Gould on Heligoland.

The Admiral inspected the Guard of Right Flank under Lance Sergeant Forbes.

Sergeant W. Graham's Squad at the Guards Depot, Caterham, in June 1943. The dress is closed neck battle dress tunics. It is interesting to note that the superintendent sergeant is not wearing a sash. Guardsman Robert Maston from Grangemouth seen in the centre of this photograph is the father of Mrs White from Mid Calder who submitted this picture.

Arbon's Squad photographed at the Guards Depot, Caterham, in August 1944. Again all except the officers are wearing closed-neck tunics. The Guards depot, Caterham, was a college of excellence. All those who trained there agree that there was no military training establishment to compare with it. The late W. Macfarlane, who is seen in the back row of this photo, was called up in 1944 from the Agricultural College. This squad experienced the effects of some of the first of the German V 2 bombs whilst on drill parade on this sacrosanct square which caused them to fall flat on their faces. To finally pass out from Caterham was considered a great honour.

This German tank was captured by the Second Battalion of the Scots Guards at Medenine in Tunis in 1943. Sergeant Mutch M.M. and Sergeant Stevenson are seen here viewing the tank.

B Company First Battalion in Italy was photographed looking across this valley to a village that was still in enemy hands.

The tanks of the Scots Guards supported the Highland Light Infantry through Cleve in 1945.

The Guardsmen of S. Company of the Scots Guards searched door to door for enemy snipers amidst the ruins of Monte Casino in Italy.

Scots Guards' tanks carried men of the 15th Scottish Division across Germany during the final days of the war.

Right: Guardsman Thomas Philip Greig, who was born on 9 August 1908, was killed in action in north-west France on 1 October 1944.

Below: Greig lies buried alongside several of his Scots Guards colleagues.

The Battle of Djebel Bou Aoukaz is remembered in this oil painting which shows Captain The Lord Lyell winning his Victoria Cross. Lord Lyell's Company was pinned down. To end this impasse his lordship collected the only available men, Lance Sergeant J. Robertson, Lance Corporal Laurie, Guardsman J. Chisholm and Guardsman Porter, and with them ran out into the open towards the enemy post. It turned out to be further away than it had at first appeared but, despite coming under fire from shells from an 88mm gun and a hail of bullets from a machine gun, they continued to run forward. Lord Lyell killed the German machine gunners with a grenade and Lance Sergeant Robertson also managed to kill several of the enemy before he himself was struck and died. The success of their attack was later marked by the award of the VC to Captain Lyell and Military Medals were presented to Lance Corporal Laurie and Guardsman Chisholm.

Guardsman John Moonie from Wishaw was pictured with the First Battalion Scots Guards in Trieste in 1945 where the XIII Corps under Lieutenant General Sir John Harding had the task of capturing the city. The New Zealand Division also closed in on the city under the command of Lieutenant General Sir Bernard Freyberg VC and accepted its surrender, but the Scots Guards shared the honour and were selected to represent Britain by marching through the streets. Guardsman Mooney was pictured at the transit staging camp at Trieste.

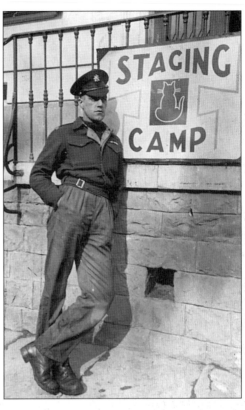

Guardsman Ralph Hendry of G Company, Second Battalion is seen here in a support vehicle in Holland at the end of the war in 1945.

G Company of the Second Battalion of the Scots Guards ended the war in the Netherlands where this group photograph was taken in 1945.

Sergeant Ernie Attack, a signals operator in the Third Tank Battalion, and Sergeant William Stewart, a Battalion HQ tank driver, were photographed at Asheberg, Plon, Schleswig-Holstein, in 1945. Ernie became a Colour Sergeant by the end of the war and was in the Colour Party which proudly returned the Battalion colours to Wellington Barracks when it was disbanded. Later in civilian life he became a painter and decorator in Penicuik, Mid Lothian, on the outskirts of Edinburgh, where he died in 2001.

The Scots Guards were honoured to form the Guard of Honour at the Potsdam Conference at the end of the war. They were pictured as wartime leader Winston Churchill inspected their ranks. The guard was founded by Left Flank of the Second Battalion, Scots Guards.

American President Truman was next to arrive at the Potsdam Conference and, together with Winston Churchill, walked through the ranks of the Scots Guardsmen.

The Soviet Union was represented by Joseph Stalin.

Great Britain's new Labour Prime Minister Clement Atlee was photographed inspecting the Guard of Honour.

Z1 Demonstration Platoon of the Scots Guards were led by pipers when they marched through the streets of Caernarvon in the VE Parade on Sunday 13 May 1945. One of the pipers played with his right hand and the other with his left!

Eyes rights! The Z1 Demonstration Platoon looked their smartest at this VE Parade in Caernarvon.

The Scots Guards were photographed at historic Caernarvon Castle. This group picture taken on 13 May 1945 shows Z1 Company of the Battle Training School at Llandwrog, which had been established in 1943. The advance party which set up the school was under the command of Captain Vesrey and the RSM was Freddy Archer, who was well known for demanding no less than 110 per cent from each man in training. Sergeant Major Thornton was also in the advance party, which moved originally from Pirbright, Surrey.

The Demonstration Platoon of Z1 Company of the Scots Guards was photographed at Warren Camp, Llandwrog, in August 1945.

The pipes and drums of the Training Battalion, Scots Guards photographed on 16 April 1945. The picture was taken at Hanelli Barracks, Hubblerath, during a visit from the Duke of Gloucester who posed with the men.

The corps of drums and pipe band of the First Battalion, Scots Guards, took part in the Remembrance Day Parade in Pola, a part of the Trieste Enclave, in November 1946. Pola became part of Italy before finally being ceded to Yugoslavia. The salute was taken by Brigadier M.D. Erskine DSO with Lieutenant Colonel C.I.H. Dunbar DSO, Commanding Officer leading the Battalion. The Corps of Drums was led by Drum Major 'Spud' Thomson and in charge of the Pipe Band was Pipe Major 'Curly' Roe.

Sergeant J. Currie's Squad at Caterham in 1946. It was taken at K Company Lines. There were around thirty men in this Company at the start of training.

No.5 Platoon, L Company, Scots Guards were pictured in January 1947.

The drums of First Battalion Scots Guards were pictured at Montebello Trotting Race Course, Trieste, in 1947 at the end of the two years which the Regiment spent there for political rather than military reasons after the end of the Second World War. This area marked the southern end of the Iron Curtain and the threat from Communism.

The First Battalion's Pipe Band and Corps of Drums was pictured at Rossetti Barracks, Trieste, in 1947. Front row, from left to right: Drummer Soppit, Piper Miller, Piper MacDonald, Drummer Glen, -?-, and Captain P.E.G. Balfour, Drum Major Thompson, Colonel Johnson, DSO, Pipe Major 'Curly' Roe, Drummer Gregg, Drummer Wells, Piper R. Kilgour, Piper Strachan. Second row, left to right: Drummers R. Fish, J. Morrison, C. Wright, A. Walker, J. Tyrall, B. Hope, M. Powell, A. Walker, A. Glasgow, W. Fielding, S. McPake, T. Hagan, J. Stutt, A. McDonald. Third Row, from left to right: Drummers D. Syme, T. Barrett, J. Paton, K. Shell, W. Watson, D. Duncan, P. Ellis, D. Kirk, B. Williams. Fourth Row: Piper J. Keddie, Piper J. Explain, Drummer D. Craig, Drummer B. Mackie, Piper W. Penman, Piper T. Dick and, at the top, Piper J. Kilgour.

Four

The War in Malaya

The end of the Second World War did not end strife throughout the world unfortunately and the men of the Second Battalion were soon posted abroad again to help deal with the troubles in Malaya. They arrived in Singapore where the colours were paraded through the streets of the then British colony.

Left Flank Three Inch Mortar Team were photographed in action at Pahang in Malaya. Although the Battalion had left Chelsea Barracks in London with a skeleton Two Inch Mortar Platoon, the mortars were handed in at Nee Soon and only later at Selerang did the mortar men finally come into their own. Captain Priaulx ran a short training course before the move to Pahang, where Left Flank performed the first shoot on a thirty-strong bandit camp in the jungle.

Lieutenant Colonel Sanderson addressed F Company in Malaya during Operation Lemon.

This magnificent specimen of a tiger was shot by Sergeant Duff of Left Flank at Trolak in February, 1951.

Lieutenant Colonel J.S. Sanderson was photographed visiting an F Company Patrol base accompanied by Major G.P. Burnett and 2nd Lieutenant the Hon. P. Lindsay.

Major Fane-Gladwin and his draft training staff at Batu Arang in the jungle of Malaya.

Major Mostyn and 2nd Lieutenant Knollys aboard a Left Flank scout car during the campaign in Malaya.

These six-footers of Right Flank succeeded in killing ten Communist terrorists in a battle during the Malaya Campaign on 28 March 1951. They are seen here posing with fixed bayonets for a recruiting poster.

This Iban tracker had Scots
Guards stars tattooed on his back.

Lieutenant Colonel A.K. Cameron of Second Battalion, Scots Guards was pictured with his Sten gun at Kapar Bharn.

Battalion sports were held at Coronation Park, Kuala Lumpur, and Headquarter Company B Team won the inter-company shield. Both team events were won by the Wing, the relay by HQ B Team and the tug of war by HQ A. First places were taken by Captain M.P. De Klee, Drill Sergeant Gibson, Guardsman Gibson, Guardsman Woods, Lieutenant Corporal Whitelaw and Guardsman Steele. In this photograph the Viscount Dalrymple is seen presenting the Battalion football cup to Sergeant Mudie at Kuala Kubu in July 1950.

Opposite: Guardsman Rae of the Signal Platoon was pictured on Listening Patrol at a base in the Malayan jungle. The campaign against the terrorists in Malaya was a testing time for the Signals Platoon. The ideal country for signallers is flat and featureless with no vegetation more than a few inches high growing in a dry temperate climate. Malaya was the entire opposite with high hills covered by tall jungle growing in the dampest of conditions. With time and patience and plenty of practice, however the Scots Guards Signals Patrol overcame these problems.

Above: This cartoon poked fun at the Scots Guards' uncomfortable time in the dense steamy jungles of Malaya with the caption, 'Y'know Bottomley, I've a ghastly feeling we will have to wear this jungle green stuff after all!'

Left: General Sir Michael Gow GCB, DI was still a major when he was photographed with Padre the Rev. Dr D.E. Whiteford CBE at the beach in Malacca on the Malaya Peninsula .

Above: The Transport Platoon of the Second Battalion was forty-eight-strong including all ranks when it left Chelsea Barracks for duties in Malaya. The Battalion was informed that it would be jeep borne and that the establishment would be in the neighbourhood of one hundred and fifty vehicles. In the panic over the presumed shortage of drivers a five day course was hurriedly arranged at Pirbright, Bordon and London to train more men. The men who attended this 'crash' course served successfully with the Platoon for the whole of its service in Malaya.

Right: Major Michael Gow, later General Gow, was pictured with Viscount Melgund at Malacca while enjoying some R&R in the Malaysian coastal resort after a spell in the jungle.

This group of Scots Guardsmen was photographed in front of the Sergeants' Mess at Kuala Kubu Bharu in 1949. Third from the left is Quarter Master Alex Greenwood.

G Company headquarters at Kuala Kubu Bharu had originally been a school.

During the three years from 1948 until 1951 that the Second Battalion Scots Guards spent in Malaya during operations against the Communist terrorists, six officers and eight other ranks lost their lives. Three of their graves are pictured here, including those of 2nd Lieutenant J.A. Forbes Leith, Guardsman D. Moore and Guardsman K. Holland. General Harding summed up the Battalion's achievements in Malaya when he wrote, 'In all their operations all ranks have displayed courage and endurance of the highest order. In addition, they have shown a fine spirit of co-operation and good comradeship with all those with whom they have worked. They have confounded critics and proved again, if further proof were necessary, that there is nothing Guardsmen cannot achieve when they put their minds to it.'

Pipe Major J. McKenzie, Second Battalion Pipe Band is seen on the occasion of his retiral presentation which took place in Batu Arang, Malaya, in 1949. Later he enlisted as Pipe Major of the Royal Canadian Air Force Pipe Band.

Service given by the cooks of Second Battalion during the Regiment's stay in Malaya was recognised when this picture of them was taken at Selerany Barracks, Changie, on the outskirts of Singapore in 1949. Seen in the front row are Captain Alex Greenwood, Major P.F. Fane-Gladwyn, second in command of the battalion, and the master cook who is thought to have been Warrant Officer McMillan.

The Second Battalion took part in the Remembrance Day Service at Selerang Barracks, Singapore, in November 1949. The band of the Seaforth Highlanders also took part.

During R&R from the jungle bashing the drums of the Second Battalion were photographed at Changi in 1949. They include Bass Drummer A. 'Tobby' Bradshaw, Drummer Stephen Roy, Drummer Alex K. Morrison, his brother Drummer Adam Morrison and Sergeant George West. Alex, Adam and George were all former pupils of Queen Victoria School, Dunblane. On demob Alex returned to become drumming instructor at his old school which still provides boarding education of the children of servicemen and women and is now co-educational.

SS *Empire Trooper* transported the Second Battalion of the Scots Guards to and from Malaya, the voyage taking four long weeks. She was finally sent to the breakers yard and scrapped at Cairnryan, near Stranraer, during the 1960s.

Five

The Regiment on Parade and on Duty

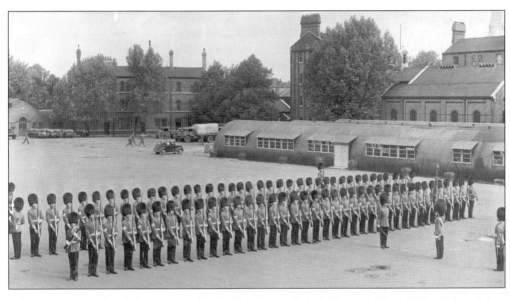

When Trooping the Colour took place in London in 1948, Second World War Nissen Huts were still to be seen. This photo shows the Second Battalion Scots Guards escort to the colour at the rehearsal at Chelsea Barracks for the King's Birthday Parade. The officers were David Ogilvy, Angus Ogilvy and RSM Fraser. The ceremony derives from the fact that in the past the colours of each Regiment were carried in battle as a rallying point for the soldiers. To ensure that all of the men recognised the colours they were trooped through the ranks. Prior to 1700 each Regiment had a colour for each Company but, by the end of the eighteenth century, each Battalion had only two colours, the Regimental Colour and the Queen's Colour. The ceremony of Trooping the Colour dates back to this time. It marks the Queen's official birthday each year in June. Each Regiment of foot guards takes a turn to troop its colour, whilst the members of the other Regiments of foot guards and the Household Cavalry also take part in the colourful ceremony.

The first ever Edinburgh Tattoo at the castle in August 1949 featured this contingent of Scots Guards who travelled north from Pirbright to take part. Top row, from left to right: R. Bruce, L. Robinson, J. Alan, -?- Morrison, E. Greenwood, A. MacNeil, -?-, R. Wadsworth, and G. Chadwick. Middle row: -?-, J. Wells, E. Morton, B. Steadman, -?-, -?-, C. Thompson, -?-, -?-, N. Dodd, and F. Simpson. Front row: S. Wyldbore, -?-, K. Green, Corporal -?-, Sergeant -?-, -?-, Sergeant Richie, S. Young and P. Cartland.

Lance Corporal Bob Fish, Lance Sergeant Johnny Walsh and Lance Sergeant Hal Scroton of the Corps of Drums, Second Battalion Scots Guards, enjoyed a visit to the Festival of Britain on London's South Bank when they returned from Malaya in 1951 during the time that the Battalion was stationed at Chelsea Barracks.

Guardsman John Smith, Right Flank, was pictured on guard outside the Crown Room in Crown Square, Edinburgh Castle, in June 1951. The Scottish National War Memorial is seen in the background. The Regiment was in Edinburgh for the presentation of new colours to both battalions, but sadly because of his deteriorating health it proved impossible for King George VI to attend. Colonel of the Regiment , General The Duke of Gloucester, Earl of Ulster, KG, KT, GCB, GCMG, GCVC deputised. The two battalions later marched from the Palace to Regent Road, where, after halting for a few moments at Waterloo Place, they continued along Princes Street to the march past at the Mound which was taken by His Royal Highness. This was the first time that both battalions had been together in the Scottish capital since the eighteenth century. They were based at Milton Bridge and at Glencorse Camp, Penicuik. The First Battalion had only recently been issued with Home Service uniform consisting of scarlet tunics and bearskins. These had been mothballed during the Second World War. The task of cleaning the brass buttons and returning these items of clothing to good condition was a very formidable one, but the guardsmen took it on and perfection was achieved! The Second Battalion, which had just come home from Malaya, was still in khaki. During its stay in the city the First Battalion founded the guard at both Edinburgh Castle and the Palace of Holyrood.

On leaving Edinburgh the First Battalion moved to Colchester to join the newly reformed Third Infantry Division in extensive training while the Second Battalion went to X Company, Chelsea Barracks, London, to carry out public duties. The reforming of Third Infantry Division was made possible by the influx of National Servicemen and the Divisional Commander, Sir Hugh Stockwell, was instructed to have them fully trained by the end of 1951. Training took place in Norfolk and in August the division took part in an exercise called Hammer and Tongs against an enemy which was made up by Eastern Command. In November the First Battalion was ordered to Cyprus as a result of the troubles in Egypt and this photo shows the ill-fated SS *Pollock Hill*, which sank off the island in December of that year as a result of a hurricane. This resulted in her breaking in two with the loss of most of the Regimental pipe band's uniforms and instruments, signals equipment and food supplies. Sadly ten of the ship's company lost their lives. The same severe storm also hit Wemyss Keep Camp at Nicosia where most of the tents were blown away. Several Guardsmen were injured and the CO's Humber car was damaged when a shed blew down.

On a lighter note, a concert was held at Wemyss Camp and this photo shows the contribution from the Officers' Mess. On the left is Captain John Ramsay, later major, who on return to civilian life became Parish Priest at Winchburgh in West Lothian.

The Guard of Honour found by Right Flank for Sir Brian Robertson G.O.C. Middle East Land Forces. The Guard Commander was Captain John Ramsay of Right Flank. The picture was taken in the square at Government House, Nicosia, in 1951. The right hand man is Bernie Donleavy from Edinburgh and Guardsman John Smith is fourth from the right.

The inspection by Sir Brian Robertson, accompanied by Captain John Ramsay. Guardsmen Bernie Donleavy and Guardsman John Smith are again in this picture.

A Guard of Honour found by Right and Left Flanks of the First Battalion for the Governor of Cyprus in Nicosia on 15 February 1952. This was to mark the death of King George VI and the accession to the throne of Her Majesty Queen Elizabeth. The Guard Commander, Captain John Ramsay, was pictured accompanying the Governor as he inspected the guard.

From Cyprus Right Flank First Battalion embarked for Egypt. This picture was taken at Famagusta Harbour. They moved to Golf Course Camp, Port Said to begin a long hot dusty stay which tried the patience and good temper of the men to the limit. Their duty was to protect equipment and installations against organised thefts and sabotage by professional Egyptian criminals and political extremists who were paid for their work at the rate (it was alleged) of £1 per night.

Above: Scots Guardsmen posed for the photographer on top of this Centurion tank belonging to the Royal Scots Greys who paid a visit to their camp in Port Said. The Scots Guards were already familiar with the Centurions as back in the UK they had taken part in Exercise Surprise Packet.

Right: Company Commander Right Flank, Major Charles J.R. Duffin, who took command of the Battalion at Pirbright in 1953. He retired as Lieutenant Colonel in 1968. He was a most professional soldier and respected leader of men. He is remembered as having had a great sense of humour and was always ready with a joke about the most difficult or dangerous of situations. He died on 1 April 1999.

Guardsman John Smith and two other members of Right Flank, First Battalion on Suez Canal Road in Egypt while driving to Moascar, stopped for a break at the Oasis in El Kantara for a break.

Shining Parade at Golf Course, Port Said. This informal photograph shows the men of Right Flank, No.3 Platoon including, in front, Peter Gaines and Tonner. To the rear are Haines, John Smith and Corporal Rudd. The one who was camera shy could be Guardsman Dawson.

The First Battalion Tug of War team won the Middle East Forces Championship during the summer of 1952 at Port Said. Captain John Ramsay the team coach shouted on the men. Captain Ramsay came out of hospital to be represented at the final and was rushed back to hospital as soon as the victorious final pull had taken place. This team never lost a pull, having beaten the Royal Navy, the Royal Marines and the Third Paratroop Regiment. The anchor man was Guardsman Gray from Arbroath and Guardsman John Smith is third from the anchor on the rope.

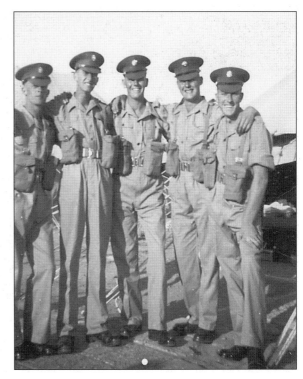

Still in Egypt the following members of 3 Platoon, Right Flank, Lance Corporal Rudd, -?-, -?-, Guardsman Smith and Guardsman Naismith pictured in 1952.

Guardsman Smith and Guardsman Dawson of 3rd Platoon, Right Flank, were photographed in Amman, Trans Jordan in 1952. Five men of Right Flank, First Battalion, spent the summer with the Arab Legion in Trans Jordan. They travelled to Amman via the Suez Canal to Fayid on the Bitter Lakes, where they spent two nights waiting for an RAF plane. The first available plane was a Valletta transport plane taking supplies to Aqaba, where a British Battalion was stationed. There were no seats when they boarded and they spent the flight sitting on sides of beef.

Lance Corporal Harry Scott and Guardsman John Smith stand on either side of an Arab Legionnaire.

Guardsman Wait walking out in Port Fuad, the European quarter of Port Said.

Pipers led the Scots Guards on their way from Golf Course Camp, Port Said, to an exercise in the Sinai Desert.

The Coronation of Her Majesty Queen Elizabeth was celebrated with this parade in which the First Battalion participated. Drum Major Grigg is pictured beginning a turn. The bandsmen in the all-white uniforms were the East Surrey Regiment. The Groundkeepers, one of whom is seen in the foreground on the left, were provided by Garrison Headquarters.

The pipes and drums of the First Battalion Scots Guards mounted guard in Moascar, halfway down the Suez Canal.

110

Sergeant Fraser, Lance Corporal Fleming and Guardman Nairn posed with their dhobi wallah, who always made an excellent job of doing their laundry!

Inspection at Moascar prior to the guardsmen being posted to their duty points. Moascar was a very large camp at Ismailia where the areas covered by the Third Infantry Division and the First Infantry Division met.

Inspection of the pipers at Moascur was undertaken by Adjutant Captain N.G. Ramsay.

Band practice in Egypt in 1953.

Dog Handler, Guardsman Ian Nairn from Arbroath was pictured with his dog Butch at Port Said in 1953, Butch became Regimental Mascot and remained with Guardsman Nairn when the Regiment returned to the UK where he became a well known character. This picture was used for a recruiting poster.

The pipes and drums at Moascur, with Commanding Officer, Lieutenant Colonel T.F.R. Bulkeley and Adjutant Captain N.G. Ramsay.

Guardsmen James Purdie and Mortimer were pictured at the Guards Depot, Pirbright, in 1953. Guardsman Purdie later joined Lothian and Peebles Constabulary and was stationed at Blackburn near Bathgate, West Lothian.

After the Queen's Birthday Parade Trooping the Colour at Dusseldorf in Germany, Pipe Sergeant Tommy Marshall, Drum Sergeant Bob Fish and Sergeant Groom Ted Lydiate enjoyed a drink outside the Sergeants' Mess.

No.22 Platoon, Scots Guards was pictured at Pirbright Camp, Brookwood, Surrey. Pirbright was originally the depot for Guards Regiment recruits, but because of cutbacks and the reduced size of the army they now have to share it with recruits from other regiments.

Warrant Officers and Sergeants posed with the Duke of Gloucester at Llanelli Barracks, Hubblerath, Germany, in 1955.

K Company Scots Guards Cross Country Team.

The pipe band of the Scots Guards was pictured playing in the streets of Falkland, Fife, outside the little town's famous royal palace, home of the Crichton-Stuart family. In 1649 King Charles I was executed in London. That same year the Regiment, which was then known as the Irish Companies, returned from Ireland. The following year in 1650, the Regiment welcomed King Charles II on his arrival from France. The King saw the Regiment as his Lyfe Guard of Foot and he appointed Argyle's son, Lord Lorn, to be its second Colonel. On 22 July that year the Regiment was presented with new colours at a ceremony at Falkland Palace, which was a favoured seat of the Scottish courts since the reign of King James V. On 30 September 1950, three hundred years later, a detachment of the First Battalion visited the palace (which is now cared for by the National Trust for Scotland) and laid up a pair of old colours of the Second Battalion, which was then serving in Malaya.

Seen here on that same occasion on 30 September 1950 is the detachment of Guardsmen entering Falkland Palace to lay up the two colours in the chapel.

The ceremony at which the colours were handed over to the care of Major Michael Crichton-Stuart took place in the grounds of the Palace. This picture shows the inspection of the Guard of Honour on the lawns of Falkland Palace. From left to right: Simon Younger, Major Michael Crichton-Stuart, Master of Falkland, Captain Ossy Prianlx, Colonel The Lord Stair and Sergeant Woods, who was the right-hand man.

During the time of National Service, after their two years in the army, Guardsmen were still required to return each year for fifteen-day refresher camps, known as Z Training. This photograph was taken at Bodney South Camp, Thetford, Norfolk. Amongst those in the picture in front of the Nissen hut are Guardsman Harry Bremner, Guardsman Scott Wait and Guardsman John Smith.

Accompanied by Brigadier Kim Ross, Her Majesty Queen Elizabeth stopped to speak to Guardsman Charles Mitchell, when she paid a royal visit to Redford Barracks, Edinburgh, in 1968.

Drum Major Nicky Taylor and Drum Sergeant Bob Fish of the Second Battalion are seen here at Duisberg Railway Station in Germany in 1954 when they bid farewell to their friends in the Second Battalion Coldstream Guards which was then returning to the UK. These two members of the Corps of Drums will be very well remembered by many Guardsmen who served in the Second Battalion and indeed by those in the First Battalion.

Her Majesty Queen Elizabeth inspected this guard of honour of the First Battalion Scots Guards at Balmoral Castle in 1968. This photograph was taken by the late Captain Tony Philipson, who was in charge of recruiting in Scotland. The Guard Commander was Major Philip Erskine.

Argentinean forces invaded the Falkland Islands in April 1982. The 2nd Battalion Scots Guards were warned to be ready for service in a task force, which was to be shipped to the South Atlantic to retake the British islands. The Battalion under the command of the 5th Infantry Brigade embarked on the 70,000 ton liner QE2 at Southampton on 12 May. Once aboard ship, training was intense and the men had to familiarise themselves with new weapons. Each Sunday the Padre held a service of worship, attended by the whole Battalion. After a voyage of over two weeks, on 28 May at South Georgia the Battalion crossed over to the 45,000 ton liner *Canberra* and arrived at San Carlos in the Falklands on 2 June where this photograph was taken.

On the night of 5-6 June in appalling weather conditions and driving rain the Battalion moved to Bluff Cove, where this photograph was taken on 8 June.

From Bluff Cove they moved up to their objective, Mount Tumbledown. The attack was launched in the early hours of 14 June and, after a very intense battle lasting ten hours, the Battalion succeeded in taking its objective. During the fighting the Battalion lost eight men killed and forty wounded. The Battalion was awarded eight decorations, whilst fourteen officers and men were mentioned in dispatches. This picture shows members of G Company in celebratory mood on top of Mount Tumbledown.

Members of the Signals Platoon relaxing in camp at Port Stanley towards the end of the campaign. The participation of the Battalion clearly did much to lead to the surrender of the Argentineans.

Padre for the 2nd Battalion Scots Guards, Rev. Lindsay Marnoch, was pictured in conversation with the Colonel of the Regiment the Duke of Kent in Northern Ireland during the Troubles in 1988.

The Padre, Rev. Lindsay Marnoch, is seen with a Scots Guardsman on the helicopter pad in Bessbrook, Northern Ireland, during a tour of South Armagh in 1987 or 1988. The Rev. Lindsay Marnoch has since left the army and is now engaged in broadcasting in London.

Guardsman Richard Mitchell is seen on duty in Oman in 1993. Guardsman Mitchell comes from Penicuik in Mid Lothian.

This photo shows Guardsmen McDonald and Hunter and Sergeant J. Brown of the Second Battalion in the cookhouse at Springfield Road Police Station, Northern Ireland, in 1971.

Members of the First Battalion are seen here mounting guard at Edinburgh Castle in 1967. This was the first occasion since 1951 that the Scots Guards had carried out public duties in home service clothing at Edinburgh Castle.

The Korean Honour Guard is a unique organisation. This Company carries out public duties which are set out by the United States Army under the auspices of the United Nations. The Honour Guard is billeted in Yongsan Barracks, Seoul, which is the United Nations Headquarters in South Korea. The Honour Guard was comprised of a United Nations Company Headquarters and one Platoon (founded in turn by each British Army Battalion) which was based in Hong Kong for a two to three-month period. The Platoon was also made up of a small number of men from other nations. Seen in this photograph is an United Nations Platoon founded from F Company , the Second Battalion which was stationed in Hong Kong and was attached to the First Battalion the Irish Guards in 1971. The photograph was taken in front of the Eight Army HQ in Seoul. In the back row are four Thailand soldiers, two Turkish soldiers and the remainder are Scots Guardsmen. Third from left in the front row is George Davidson from Inverness. Apart from the Guardsman third from left, who is sadly deceased, all are still alive and five are living in the Highlands.

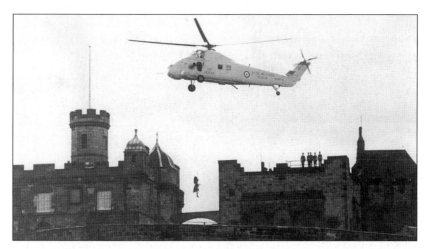

At the famous Edinburgh Military Tattoo, the lone piper was to have been flown onto the battlements suspended from the helicopter seen in this picture. The Army School of Piping, however, did not take kindly to the idea of risking one of their top pipers for such a stunt. In the end the problem was solved when Major Campbell Graham of the Scots Guards was detailed to take the place of the piper. Dressed in the uniform of a piper with kilt and plaid he dangled from the rope below the helicopter each night. As his kilt blew high he also always took the precaution of wearing pants and grabbed this eye-catching opportunity to promote the Regiment by having sewn onto them the bold slogan, 'Join The Scots Guards'. As soon as he landed atop the castle he slipped quickly into the shadow of the battlements and was replaced by the actual piper with the cheering audience never any the wiser.

Her Majesty Queen Elizabeth, Colonel-In-Chief of the Scots Guards, with the Colonel, the Duke of Kent, the Lieutenant Colonel, the two Commanding Officers and the Regimental Sergeant Majors of the Battalions of the Regiment. Also pictured are the Regimental Adjutant and two Adjutants of the Battalions with the officers of the Colour Party. This picture was taken after the 350th anniversary parade in the grounds of Holyrood Palace, Edinburgh on 24 June 1992. The colours of the First and Second Battalions are seen in the background.

The members of the Regiment and the men of the Scots Guards Association marched past Her Majesty Queen Elizabeth, Colonel-in-Chief, in Holyrood Park, Edinburgh, on the occasion of the 350th anniversary of the founding of the Regiment on 24 June 1992.

The 350th anniversary of the formation of the Scots Guards was marked by this parade at Holyrood Park in 1992. The Duke of Edinburgh is seen with Lieutenant Colonel Spicer talking with members of the Scots Guards Association.

A training exercise at Lydd Camp, Kent, in preparation for service in Northern Ireland was as realistic as it could possibly be made.

The First Battalion was stationed in Ballykiner in 1999 during the troubles in Northern Ireland. and was always kept busy with the ever-changing situation. During this policing situation the pipers all played an active role in the peace-keeping duties which the battalion fulfilled. This photograph shows Lance Sergeant B. Herriot, Lance Corporal S. McKay and Piper R. McRindle, all of the Pipes and Drums of the First Battalion on duty at Drumcree, which was well known as a flash point. The famous church at Drumcree was a focal point for demonstrations in Northern Ireland and forms the backdrop for this picture of Guardsmen on duty in the troubled Province.

The Regimental Band of the Scots Guards marched down the main street in Brechin, Angus, on the occasion of the annual gathering of the Regiment in September 2001.

The gathering brought together the Regiment as a family with both active and retired Guardsmen present. At Brechin Cathedral, the Earl and Countess of Dalhousie were photographed with Colonel J.M. Claveny, watched by many spectators including many children who from their interest may someday hope to join the Scots Guards and continue the proud traditions of this fine Scottish Regiment.